Cambridge English Readers

Level 4

Series editor: Philip Prowse

But Was it Murder?

Jania Barrell

CAMBRIDGE
UNIVERSITY PRESS

PUBLISHED BY THE PRESS SYNDICATE OF THE UNIVERSITY OF CAMBRIDGE
The Pitt Building, Trumpington Street, Cambridge, United Kingdom

CAMBRIDGE UNIVERSITY PRESS
The Edinburgh Building, Cambridge CB2 2RU, UK
40 West 20th Street, New York, NY 10011-4211, USA
477 Williamstown Road, Port Melbourne, VIC 3207, Australia
Ruiz de Alarcón 13, 28014 Madrid, Spain
Dock House, The Waterfront, Cape Town, South Africa

http://www.cambridge.org

© Cambridge University Press 2000

First published 2000
Fifth printing 2003

This book is in copyright. Subject to statutory exception and
to the provisions of relevant collective licensing agreements,
no reproduction of any part may take place without
the written permission of Cambridge University Press.

Printed in the United Kingdom at the University Press, Cambridge

Typeset in 12/15pt Adobe Garamond [CE]

ISBN 0 521 78359 3

Contents

Characters

Detective Inspector Rod Eliot: Policemen at
Detective Constable Jamie Bowen: New Cross police
Police Constable Drewitt: station, London.

Sally Eliot: Rod Eliot's wife.

Micky Eliot: Rod Eliot's son.

Alex Forley: owner of an antique furniture shop.

Mr and Mrs Crowther: Forley's neighbours.

Amanda Grant: Forley's girlfriend.

Philip Wilver: Forley's doctor.

Lisa Wilver: his wife.

Mrs Brook: a cleaner.

Linda Scott: manager of Forley's antique shop.

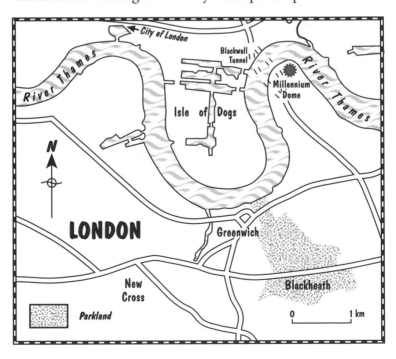

Chapter 1 *Missing The Queen's Head*

Detective Inspector Rod Eliot was watching the rain running down his office window. He looked at his watch. 6.30. Time to leave the mountain of papers on his desk and go to The Queen's Head pub across the road.

'But only one beer,' he told himself. 'I don't want to be stopped by some junior policeman for drunk driving. Then I'll have to go home to an empty house.'

Just as he was leaving the office, the phone rang. He turned back automatically and picked it up. He half hoped it might be his wife.

'Sorry to disturb you, sir,' said Detective Constable Jamie Bowen. 'But we've got a bit of a problem.'

'So have I,' said Eliot. 'I shouldn't be here. Ask Inspector Merryon.'

'Sorry, sir,' said Bowen, 'but Inspector Merryon hasn't arrived yet. He phoned to say his car is stuck in a traffic jam in Hackney. He probably won't be here for at least an hour.'

Eliot hit the top of his desk angrily. The lights from The Queen's Head looked so inviting. But in the street below people were crowded into shop doorways, trying to escape from the rain. The water poured onto the street and was thrown up again by the lines of cars moving slowly away from the centre of London.

'All right, Bowen,' he said. 'You'd better tell me about it then. What is it?'

'We've just had a report of a death, sir. And there's a gun.'

This was the last thing Eliot wanted to hear. He had been in a bad mood all day. He usually liked Friday because of the weekend ahead, when he could spend time with his wife Sally and eight-year-old son Micky. Micky was crazy about football, and Eliot always took him to watch West Ham on Saturdays when they played at home. This weekend would be different, though. Eliot had to work, and Sally had taken Micky to her parents' house in Brighton for two nights. He had argued with her that morning.

'Stop shouting,' she had said. 'You're just angry because you don't want us to go away. Why can't you admit it?'

She was right, but knowing this only made him more angry. He had left the house without saying goodbye to her.

He had tried to ring several times to say sorry, but there was no answer. Now she would be at her parents' house. And she could not speak to him openly there because they would be listening.

'I knew this would be a bad day from the moment I woke up,' he told Bowen. 'All right. We'll have to go. Where is it?'

'Blackheath, I'm afraid, sir.'

Eliot sighed. Blackheath was only six kilometres from New Cross police station. But at this time on a Friday night there was so much traffic that the journey could take over an hour.

Eliot could not think of a worse way of spending Friday evening, especially as he had to be in his office early next morning. Why did everyone try to leave London at the same time? One day the whole city would be stuck in one big traffic jam. Already the traffic moved more slowly than it had a hundred years ago. It was madness.

'Meet me downstairs in ten minutes, Bowen,' he said. 'Oh, and there'll have to be medical reports. Check that someone's told a doctor and the pathologist.'

Eliot turned away from the window. Well, at least Sally and Micky weren't waiting for him at home. He had better phone them now. It might be his last chance this evening.

Sally's father picked up the phone. 'Hello Rod. Pity you can't be here. The weather's beautiful. How's the job?'

Eliot made himself chat politely for a few minutes and then asked to speak to Sally.

'I'm afraid she's not here,' her father said. 'She's taken Micky for a walk. He couldn't wait to see the sea. Any message for her?' Eliot couldn't believe his bad luck.

'Just say I'm pleased they've arrived safely,' he said. 'And give her my love. I'll ring again tomorrow.'

He put down the phone and took one last look at The Queen's Head. The traffic seemed hardly to have moved. Well, at least he could get Bowen to drive.

Chapter 2   *The colour of death*

The car went forward a few metres, and then stopped again. At first Bowen had switched on the blue light and siren so that other drivers would let them pass. But there was no space for them to get through, and they had almost caused two accidents.

They were nearly in Blackheath now. The rain had stopped but the traffic seemed to be getting worse.

Blackheath Village is one of the prettiest and greenest parts of south east London. Its narrow streets are on a hill with pleasant views, unusual houses and many restaurants. Large areas of grass separate the village from the main road. Here children play and lovers wander, and families walk with their dogs.

Tomorrow night there would be crowds, as it was November 5, Guy Fawkes Day. Thousands of people would come to the Blackheath firework show if they weren't having parties in their own gardens. Some of these parties seemed to have started already. The sky was full of the sounds and colours of fireworks exploding above their heads.

Eliot thought about his son with a sudden pain. Micky would be so excited tomorrow. Eliot would have loved to bring him here.

He made himself think about his work instead.

'What do you know about this death?' he asked Bowen.

'Not much, sir. It's a white man in his thirties.'

'I suppose we'll find out more when we arrive. If we ever do arrive, Bowen,' added Eliot impatiently.

'Sorry, sir. I'm doing my best,' said Bowen.

Eliot wondered how Bowen would feel about seeing the dead body. It was never easy, even for himself after all these years, though he had become much harder.

Bowen was twenty-eight, ten years younger than Eliot, and had worked with him since first joining the police. His parents were rich and he had been to Cambridge University. This had worried Eliot at first. But Bowen was honest and intelligent and a good policeman. Eliot now had a high opinion of him, though he did not often show it.

But there was one thing about Bowen which Eliot could not understand: he was always falling in love with the wrong women. They were either married, or not interested in him, or totally crazy. Recently he had started asking Eliot for advice when they were in the car together.

'All that education, and he can't get a girlfriend. What a waste!' Eliot thought. 'And he's not bad looking, with those dark eyes and all that black curly hair.'

Eliot knew how lucky he was to be happily married himself. He was sorry for Bowen and angry with himself for arguing with Susan that morning. He wished she had been there when he phoned.

At last they turned off the main road and stopped outside a small but beautiful eighteenth century house at the end of a quiet street. Lights were shining from all the windows. Eliot got out and stretched his legs. Normally he would have looked forward to seeing the inside of such a lovely building.

A young policeman opened the door. He looked pale, and seemed very pleased to see them.

'Evening, sir. Evening, sir,' he said, looking at each of them. 'My name's Drewitt. The, er, body's through here.'

They followed him through a hall with a deep red Persian carpet, past some beautiful wooden stairs and into a sitting room at the back. A fire was burning in the fireplace, and lamps on low tables threw a warm light over the curtains and walls and antique furniture. An open piano stood by the window, with music on it and a half-filled glass of red wine.

Eliot's attention was caught by a dark shape on the wall beside one of the armchairs. It was the same colour as the carpet in the hall. At first it seemed the only ugly thing in the room. But then Eliot looked down at the chair. He quickly looked away again.

It was a man's body. But he only knew it was a man from its shape and the clothes it wore. Not enough of the face remained to show what sex it had been. It sat in a chair with its back to the window. A gun lay beside it on the floor.

Eliot made himself look again. The hands were long, with thin, well-shaped fingers. Piano-playing hands. There was a thick gold ring on the third finger of the right hand. So he wasn't married, though he could be divorced. His clothes looked expensive, as you would expect in a house like this.

In the few seconds it took for these thoughts to cross Eliot's mind, Bowen had taken out his notebook and started questioning Drewitt.

'Bowen's becoming as hard as me,' Eliot thought. 'Not like young Drewitt there. He's as white as a sheet.'

'Any idea who he is?' Bowen asked Drewitt.

Drewitt was obviously having difficulty speaking. 'Well, sir,' he said at last, 'the house belongs to a Mr Alex Forley. His neighbours called us. Mr and Mrs Crowther. They live next door. He normally had tea with them on Fridays, and they got worried when he didn't come this afternoon as he'd been feeling ill. He didn't answer his doorbell, so they got into the back garden and saw him through the window. The doctor's already been and gone, sir.'

'Yes,' said Bowen. 'He wouldn't have needed to stay long. Anyone can see the man's dead.'

'We'll have a word with the Crowthers later,' Eliot said. 'I'd better wait here till the pathologist arrives. Bowen, why don't you talk to the other neighbours. See if they can tell us anything interesting.'

There was a ring at the doorbell. Two more policemen came in and started taking photographs of the dead body, but it was another half hour before the pathologist arrived. He was a short fat cheerful man, who looked as if nothing could annoy him.

'Hello, Eliot. Good to see you again. Sorry it's taken me so long to get here. The traffic's awful. I expect it's all these Guy Fawkes Night parties. I don't see why they can't wait till tomorrow. But still, there's a bright side to everything. I managed to hear all of Mahler's Eighth Symphony on the way here. A great recording. Life's too short to worry. Don't you agree, Eliot?'

Eliot did not answer.

'I'm sure *he'd* agree with me, if he could,' the pathologist said cheerfully, pointing to the body on the chair. 'Unless, of course, it was suicide. Well, I'd better take a look at him. I don't expect you want to stay here all night chatting.'

He opened his bag, and Eliot decided to go outside.

Chapter 3 *Just friends*

Eliot walked around the house. The garden was well cared for. He could see that even in the dark. The grass was cut, late roses were flowering on two walls, and the stone paths were clean and tidy. The windows of the sitting room were French windows, which opened like doors on to the garden outside.

'A lovely room. Perfect in summer,' he thought.

Automatically, he went up to the French windows and tried to open them. He was quite surprised to find they were unlocked.

'I suppose this is how Drewitt got in,' he thought. 'I wonder why they're open, though. It hasn't been the sort of weather for enjoying the garden. But it probably doesn't mean anything. Some people like to go out in all weathers to look at their roses.' He saw there was a gate in the back wall of the garden, which looked new. Sally wanted one of these in their own garden, so that they did not have to carry plants through the house.

He went back inside and looked in every room. The bathroom told him immediately that Forley lived alone. One toothbrush stood in a mug next to a shaving brush, and there was a single towel in a ring on one wall. Eliot could see the letters AF on one corner. The other rooms were all as beautifully arranged as the sitting room. Forley obviously cared about his house very much, more than many single men.

'A man with a lot of taste and a lot of money,' Eliot thought. 'A lucky man. Except that his luck stopped today. I wonder what other people thought of his luck.'

He went downstairs and waited till the pathologist had finished his work.

'Can you tell me anything yet?' he asked him.

'Well, I don't think he's been dead very long. But I can't say any more until I've examined him properly. And I don't think you'll get the report until Monday. I couldn't tell you what time, I'm afraid. We're so busy at the moment. The work's increasing, and they're cutting the number of staff. The world's going mad. But I know you won't mind waiting, Eliot. You're a family man, aren't you? You'll have much more pleasant things to think about at the weekend.'

He went out of the door with a smile, just as Bowen walked in.

'Did you find out anything interesting?' Eliot asked.

'Not really, sir,' said Bowen. 'A lot of people were out. The ones I spoke to have all moved here quite recently, and don't seem to know anything about him. A few people mentioned they had sometimes seen a woman here, but no-one was very interested in him. None of them know what work he does.'

'City people!' said Eliot. 'They don't care about their neighbours. If Mr and Mrs Crowther hadn't called us, he could have been lying there for weeks before anyone noticed something was wrong. Well, we'd better go round and see them now.'

Number 20 was not as beautiful as Forley's house, Eliot thought. But there were roses growing around the front door and the front garden was bigger than Eliot's own. If he was offered a house like this he would certainly not refuse. They walked up the path and rang the bell, paying no attention to the explosions of fireworks around them.

Mr Crowther opened the door immediately. He was a white-haired man in late middle age. He stood very straight, which made him seem taller than he really was. His face was lined, but he looked strong and healthy, though his hands were shaking.

'What happened to poor Alex?' he asked.

'We don't know yet, sir,' said Eliot. 'But we'd like to ask you and your wife some questions.'

Crowther controlled himself with an effort, and led them into a large sitting room. Eliot's attention was caught by the pictures which covered one of the walls. They were an interesting mix of colours, mostly blues and greens, and had obviously been painted by the same person. Mr Crowther introduced his wife, Catherine, and Eliot felt immediately that she was the painter.

She was a beautiful woman with blonde hair and lovely green eyes. It was difficult to tell her age, but she was certainly much younger than her husband. Eliot guessed she was in her forties. There was no colour in her face, but she answered his questions calmly enough. A strong and intelligent woman, Eliot thought.

'No, Inspector, we haven't seen Alex since a week ago,' she told him. 'We usually meet on Friday afternoons, either here or at his house. We've done it for years. He phoned this morning from his shop in Greenwich to say he was coming. He and I were going to play some music together. We often do that. It's a pleasant way to end the week.'

'I'm sure it is,' said Eliot, remembering his own Friday afternoons. He turned to her husband.

'Have you known Mr Forley a long time, sir?'

'Let me see. It must be about fifteen years now, since he moved here. That was about a year after he left university. His mother had just died. She had a lot of money, and she left it all to Alex. Her death made him a very rich young man.'

'I see,' said Eliot. He let Crowther continue.

'Alex was very unhappy at first,' he began. 'His mother had been ill for some time. It was a long and unpleasant illness, and he took care of her. His father had died some years ago. She and Alex were very close. Anyway, when he came here, he had no family left. We haven't got children of our own, Inspector, and he was like a son to us.'

The age difference between Forley and Mrs Crowther could not be very big. If Forley had left university at the age of twenty-one, like most people, he would now be thirty-seven. Could she really feel like a mother towards a man of that age? Eliot looked at Mrs Crowther, and saw some embarrassment on her face.

'What time were you expecting him this afternoon?' he asked.

'He usually comes about four o'clock.' Her voice changed. 'I can't speak about him in the past tense. I can't believe he'll never come again.'

She put her face in her hands and began to cry quietly.

Chapter 4 *The sound of a shot*

'But Blackheath isn't a violent place, Inspector,' Mr Crowther said. 'We've lived here for thirty years and nothing like this has ever happened before. Of course there's a bit of stealing sometimes, but never murder. We've always felt very safe here.'

Eliot wanted to say that murder could happen anywhere, even in the nicest places. But he only said, 'Hold on, sir. We don't yet know that it was murder.'

'Then you think it looked like suicide?' Mr Crowther asked.

'That's impossible,' his wife said. 'Alex would not have killed himself. What reason could he possibly have had?'

'I don't think anything yet, Mr Crowther,' Eliot replied. 'I just have to consider all the possibilities, including accidental death.'

'Oh, the gun,' Mrs Crowther began. She stopped, and gave her husband a quick look.

There was a silence before Eliot continued.

'Can you tell us about Mr Forley's job?' he asked. 'You said he had a shop in Greenwich.'

'Forley Antiques,' she answered. 'It's one of those big antique furniture shops on Park Street, near the Royal Naval College. You must know it.'

Eliot had been there once, when he was first married, before Sally's birthday. He had seen a small table in the window which he knew she would love. With his recent salary rise, he thought he might be able to afford it. But he had been really shocked to hear the price. The young girl assistant had made him feel quite uncomfortable, and he had left quickly.

'Yes, I've been inside,' he answered. 'But I don't remember seeing Mr Forley.'

'Oh, he doesn't spend much time there,' Mrs Crowther said. 'He doesn't have to. He just chooses the furniture. There's a manager and a part-time assistant who do most of the work.'

She was talking of Forley in the present tense again, as if she could not believe he was dead. She and her husband both looked very tired. Eliot would not get much useful information from them this evening.

'We won't need to stay long,' he said. 'But I'm afraid we'll have to come back tomorrow. There are just one or two more things I need to know now. Did you notice anything unusual this afternoon?'

The two houses were not attached, and both had thick walls. But it was just possible that the sound of a gunshot next door would be heard here.

'I'm afraid I can't help you, Inspector,' said Mr Crowther. 'I was out most of the afternoon. I went for my usual walk after lunch, and I didn't get back till about ten past four. You didn't hear anything, did you, my dear?' he asked his wife.

She seemed to be choosing her words carefully. 'Well, I do remember hearing a bang while you were out. I was working and I didn't really think about it at the time. I paint pictures, Inspector, and my work takes all my attention. There are so many fireworks at the moment that

I didn't give it another thought. But I suppose it is rather unusual to hear a firework in the middle of the afternoon.'

'What time was this?' asked Eliot.

'It must have been after three o'clock,' she said. 'That's when I started painting. Probably around three thirty.'

'Where were you?' he asked.

'In the front room upstairs,' she answered. 'You can see Alex's front door from there. Oh, why didn't I pay more attention? If someone had come out of the house, I could have seen them.'

'Unless they left through the French windows,' Eliot said. 'Now, I'm afraid we'll need someone to identify the body, to be sure it is Mr Forley. You told us he had no relatives when his mother died. Did he ever marry?'

Mrs Crowther covered her face with her hands. Her husband put his arm round her, and answered for her.

'No. He had a girlfriend, though – Amanda Grant. I always thought they would get married some day. We've got her address somewhere. I'll go and get it.'

He came back into the room and handed Eliot the address.

'Please don't contact Miss Grant,' said Eliot. 'We'll give her the news ourselves.'

Eliot nodded at Bowen and they both stood up. They had all the information they were going to get that evening.

Chapter 5 *New Cross at night*

'What I don't understand,' said Bowen when they were in the car again, 'is why a beautiful woman like that would marry someone so much older than herself. What can she see in him?'

Eliot did not answer. During his ten years of marriage, he had often asked himself the same thing about Sally. But he realised the younger man had his own reason for asking the question. What Bowen really wanted to know was why some men were successful with women when he himself was not. Eliot did not know the reason. It was just luck, he supposed, and being attracted to the right kind of woman.

Eliot had seen Bowen's latest girlfriend once or twice, a photographer he had met at a wedding. She was certainly attractive, if you liked tall thin women, but she looked hard. The relationship had been going badly for some time, and she had stopped returning his phone calls. But Bowen was still mad about her. He had been coming to work with dark circles under his eyes recently. And Eliot had twice had to speak to him about being late for work.

'Crowther's obviously crazy about his wife,' Bowen said. 'But how does she feel about him? They couldn't be more different. She's musical and paints. Did you see those wonderful pictures on the wall? But he seems quite ordinary. He must be rich, though, to live in a house like that.'

Eliot let him continue talking. It was more pleasant to think about the Crowthers than the dead man. At least they were alive and still had faces you could recognise. Mrs Crowther seemed to have been especially close to Forley. He would be interested to know what her husband had thought about that. And what had she wanted to say about the gun?

A lot of questions filled his mind. They would all need answers, eventually. But he tried not to guess what these might be. The case had only just begun, and he did not yet know all the facts. It was important to keep his mind as open as possible.

Of course, it might not be a very difficult job. They would probably find that Forley had killed himself. He didn't seem to have left a note, but that wasn't so unusual these days. Eliot hoped they would not have to wait too long for the pathologist's report.

The journey back to New Cross was easier. The traffic was much lighter now, and they were only stopped by one red light. Eliot thought he might even get home in time for the news.

After Blackheath Hill, Bowen had to pay more attention to the road. Driving in many parts of London was like a competition now, with drivers trying to overtake each other as much as possible. And they did not always slow down when they saw a police car.

Suddenly, Bowen had to brake to avoid a crash. A silver-grey Mercedes had been left in the middle of the road with no lights and the engine still running.

'The kids around here!' said Eliot. 'They've got no idea of danger. It's because no-one takes care of them. I suppose stealing cars is the only fun they get, at least until they're old enough to start selling drugs.'

The week before, he had caught two young boys in a stolen car. Their father had been watching football when the police phoned, and he was very angry that he had to go to the police station before the end of the match. The boys were given a strong warning, and then allowed to go. But just two hours later they were back at the police station, with smiles on their faces. After getting home, they had gone straight out to steal another car.

This kind of thing was happening more and more these days, and it worried Eliot. The younger boy had only been ten, just two years older than Micky. What hope was there for a child like that?

Until now, he had managed to protect Micky from the worst elements of city life. But he did not know how much longer this could last. In New Cross, boys had to show they were strong, through fighting or crime. Eliot worried about his gentle son. He and Sally had been talking for a long time about moving to a safer area. He must look at house prices the next time he was in Blackheath.

It took twenty minutes for a policeman to come and take the Mercedes away.

'The owner's going to be pleased to get it back,' said Bowen. 'He's lucky it wasn't stolen by professionals. He'd never have seen it again.'

By now they had passed Goldsmith's College. The pavements were full of young people waiting outside take-away restaurants or queuing to get into music clubs. The girls looked very cold in thin dresses and jackets. It made Eliot want to turn up the heating in the car. He was lucky

Micky was a boy. If he had a daughter, he knew he would worry about her even more.

The police station was quite crowded when he went in to make his report. Friday and Saturday were always the busiest nights. Too much alcohol was drunk by young people, and many had hardly eaten more than a sandwich since breakfast. It was not surprising that they became noisy and violent. There were often fights. 'The English problem,' thought Eliot. 'We're famous for it. We even export it, on holiday and at football matches.'

He bought a take-away meal from an Indian restaurant and drove home. The news had just finished and he began to watch a comedy programme. He usually enjoyed it but today the jokes didn't seem very funny. Perhaps it was because he was tired. He had had a long day.

Normally, Eliot went to sleep as soon as his head touched the pillow, waking up after exactly eight hours, feeling fresh and lively. But tonight he kept turning from side to side, unable to relax. And when sleep finally came, it gave him no peace.

He dreamed he saw Micky and Sally in the back of a stolen Mercedes. A gun lay on the seat in front, next to the driver. Eliot watched in fear as the man went faster and faster. He shouted at him to stop. Suddenly the man turned round without slowing the car, and Eliot saw only blood instead of a face. Eliot woke up covered in sweat.

Chapter 6 *Identifying the body*

Eliot woke at 7.45 with the sun on his face. It was strange how things always seemed better in the morning. Last night's worries had completely disappeared, and he was looking forward to the day ahead.

After a quick bath, he went down to get his newspaper from the letter-box. The front page was full of stories of political bribes. He read it with interest while he was having his coffee and toast. It was nice to have a quiet breakfast, for a change. But he wondered what time he could phone Sally. It was too early now. He might wake her parents.

It was surprising how much he wanted to hear her voice. In their ten years of marriage, he had sometimes had to go away for work. He did not mind this occasionally. But she had very rarely left him, and he missed her. He supposed this was why he had slept so badly.

At the police station, Bowen was waiting outside his office.

'Any developments?' asked Eliot.

'Well, sir, we've just heard that there were several people's fingerprints in the house. But on the gun, there were only the dead man's.'

'Not a great help,' said Eliot. 'It could still be suicide. Or an accident. Or murder. Maybe someone shot him, cleaned the gun, and then put it in his hand to look like suicide. Well, we'd better see Amanda Grant and take her to look at the body. Then we'll make another visit to the Crowthers.'

Amanda Grant lived in Greenwich, which was halfway between New Cross and Blackheath. Eliot wanted to start early to avoid the crowds as much as possible.

Thousands of tourists arrived every day from the centre of London. Many were visitors to the Millennium Dome, while others came to see the famous old parts of Greenwich: the Queen's House, the Old Royal Observatory and the *Cutty Sark*, the fastest ship to bring tea from China in the nineteenth century. On Saturdays, the tourists were joined by people from other areas of London. They visited the park and the many markets around the town where you could buy almost anything, old or new.

Bowen had to park the car some distance from where Amanda Grant lived. Her house was not on a road, but looked directly out over the river, with only her garden and a public path in between. It was small, but very attractive.

'It's so quiet, we could almost be in the country,' said Eliot. 'But we're only a few minutes from the centre of Greenwich. I wonder how much this house is worth. Certainly a lot more than I could afford.'

The door was opened by a short, dark-haired woman in her late twenties, dressed in jeans and a long bright-coloured pullover. She looked rather pale and tired. She was not beautiful like Catherine Crowther, but she had an attractive face. Eliot could not remember where he had seen her face before.

'Good morning,' said Eliot. 'I'm Detective Inspector Eliot, and this is Detective Constable Bowen. We'd like to speak to Amanda Grant, if she's at home.'

'I'm Amanda Grant,' she answered. Her voice was unusually deep. 'What can I do for you, Inspector?'

'May we come in, Miss Grant?' asked Eliot. 'It would be easier to talk inside.'

She looked surprised but calmly asked them to come in. The front door opened directly into a sitting room, where bright curtains and carpets gave a warm feeling. A cat was washing itself on a chair. Through the window Eliot could see the yellow and white shapes of the Millennium Dome beside the river. In front of it a boat moved slowly towards the centre of Greenwich. Piano music was coming from a CD player next to a large desk covered with papers and books. At one end a single rose stood in a glass vase. Eliot felt very unwilling to bring the subject of death and guns into this peaceful room.

She did not say a word while he spoke, or for a long time afterwards.

'I suppose you'll want me to identify the body,' she said eventually. 'You obviously need to make sure it's Alex.' Her face showed no sign of what she was feeling.

Eliot wondered how many more strong and intelligent women they would find in Forley's life.

'Yes, I'm afraid so, Miss Grant,' he said. 'We'll take you there now, if you don't mind. After that, we'll need to ask you some questions.'

Her face was pale as she switched off the music and put on her coat. But she was quite calm as she got into the car. Could she really be as cool as she seemed?

Eliot looked at her closely as they went into the building. She still showed no sign of strong feeling. Her hands started to shake only when the body was brought out and the plastic sheet taken off. Of course, the head remained covered. If she could not be sure without seeing the face, they would have to use fingerprints and dentist's records. But he did not think this would be necessary. Anyone who knew this man would recognise those long fingers. She looked quickly at the body, and nodded at Eliot.

'You're certain?' he had to ask.

She touched the man's right hand for a moment. Then she started to cry.

No-one spoke as they drove back into Greenwich. Unusually for November, the sun was still bright, and many people were carrying their jackets over their arms.

A grey sky would have been more suitable, Eliot thought. It would have matched the sadness in Amanda Grant's eyes. She was staring straight ahead of her. She obviously did not notice the weather or Eliot's face as he turned round to look at her.

Chapter 7 *Not an easy relationship*

The cat jumped off the chair as they entered Amanda Grant's house. It went out of the room, and Bowen followed to look for the kitchen. Since joining the police he had become used to making tea in strange houses. He found most people felt better after a cup if it was strong and very sweet.

Amanda Grant took the drink and thanked him quietly. She tasted it and made a face because of the sugar, but drank it without saying anything.

She seemed quite calm again when Eliot started asking questions.

'I'm a journalist, Inspector,' she said. 'I work for a magazine called *Women in the World*. I don't suppose you've heard of it.'

But he had. Sally had started getting it, and he had looked at it occasionally, trying to understand why it interested her. Suddenly, he remembered where he had seen Amanda Grant's face. It was in the magazine every month, on the inside front page. He had noticed it because it was so much younger than the three other faces there. Obviously, she was a very successful woman.

'I'm afraid I don't have time for magazines, Miss Grant,' he answered, not completely truthfully. 'Have you known Mr Forley long?'

'Almost four years,' she said. 'We met on December 31st, at a New Year's Eve party. After that we started seeing each other quite often.'

'How often?' asked Eliot.

'Oh, several times a week,' she answered. 'But not so much recently.' She turned her face away. 'My new job takes so much of my time that he wanted me to give it up. We had lots of arguments about it. We had one the last time I saw him.'

She put her hand over her eyes.

'And when was that, Miss Grant?' Eliot asked.

'Sunday evening,' she said. 'Then I was away in Edinburgh till yesterday afternoon. I should have phoned during the week, but I was angry with him. I suppose he felt the same. I called yesterday when I got back, but he wasn't in.' Her voice seemed to change a little. 'It was Friday,' she said, 'so I supposed he'd gone to see Catherine Crowther earlier than usual.'

'But I understood he went to see both the Crowthers,' said Eliot, a little more sharply than he had intended.

'That's what Ronald Crowther likes to think,' she answered. 'He was very kind to Alex after his mother died. Alex was alone in the world and he needed Ronald's help at first. But then he got better, and his life changed. He needed Ronald less, but Ronald started to depend on him. Ronald's rather lonely. He doesn't have many friends.'

Eliot looked interested, but said nothing.

'Alex began to find Ronald rather boring,' she continued, 'though he never showed it. He hated hurting people, and he couldn't forget how kind Ronald had been to him. But Alex shared more interests with Catherine. They liked each other a lot, though Ronald never seemed jealous. Ronald's interested in sport, and Alex wasn't. But he used to pretend he was, to make the old man happy.'

'And were you jealous,' Miss Grant? Eliot wanted to ask. But this was not the right time for this question. Instead he looked thoughtfully at a photograph on her desk. It showed a tall thin man with blond hair and dark eyes which were laughing at the camera. A very handsome man. If this was Alex, it was not surprising that he was loved by women.

She followed his eyes, and nodded for the second time that day.

'Yes, that's Alex,' she said.

'Do you mind if we borrow the picture?' asked Eliot.

She gave it to him without a word.

'Is there anything more you'd like to tell us about Mr Forley?' Eliot asked. 'Anything unusual or different?'

'Well, recently he said he'd been feeling weak, and then he started getting headaches,' she replied. 'Before that, he'd never really been ill. He didn't even have a doctor until this year. I suppose that was why he got so worried about his headaches. And he had a lot of time to think about his health. Alex had a lot of money, Inspector, and he hardly needed to work. He could afford to be lazy. Some people might call that lucky, but I wouldn't be happy with a life like that.'

She looked impatient for a moment. Then she continued, 'Anyway, for some reason he got the idea that there was something seriously wrong with his health. But he wouldn't say what he thought it was. He even had some hospital tests a few weeks ago.'

'And what did they show?' asked Eliot.

'I don't know,' she answered. 'The results still hadn't arrived the last time I saw him. I kept telling him that was a good sign. If they had found anything serious, they would have told him immediately.'

'You have to wait for everything these days,' said Eliot, thinking of the pathologist's report. 'Fewer and fewer people do more and more of the work. Well, we'll need his doctor's name and address. Do you know it?'

'Philip Wilver,' she said. 'Alex had known him for years. He works in Blackheath, so when Alex needed a doctor, he was the obvious choice. He lives at 54 Pepys Road, in New Cross.'

'That's a long way from his work,' said Eliot, thinking of last night's traffic jam.

'He couldn't afford a house in Blackheath. He hasn't been a doctor for very long. His family were poor, like mine. We've both had to fight for what we've got. Unlike Alex.'

She looked at the place on the desk where Forley's photograph had been. Then she looked down. Eliot wished he could give it back to her.

'Miss Grant,' Eliot said gently. 'can you think of any reason why Mr Forley might have wanted to kill himself?'

Her face lost all its colour. She looked at Eliot helplessly, and shook her head.

'Would you like us to phone a friend for you?' Eliot asked. 'They could come and sit with you. We'll wait until they arrive.'

'Thank you, Inspector,' she said. 'But I'll be all right alone.'

Eliot and Bowen said goodbye, but she did not seem to hear them. Eliot wondered if she knew she still had her coat on.

Chapter 8   *The Blackheath bonfire*

The two men were silent for a long time, affected by Amanda Grant's sadness. Eliot had forgotten about Guy Fawkes Night until they got to the top of Blackheath Hill. No children were playing on the grass today. Instead it had a fence around it, with signs telling people to stay out. Inside the fence, there was a lot of activity.

Groups of people were studying pieces of paper and shouting instructions. Workmen were carrying fireworks of all shapes and sizes and piling them onto plastic sheets lying on the ground. In the middle, four men were building a large bonfire.

'I suppose we're lucky Forley died yesterday, and not today,' Eliot said at last. 'The traffic will be worse than ever tonight.'

'What did you think of her, sir?' Bowen asked. 'At first she seemed so cool, like one of those hard career women.'

'I liked her,' said Eliot. 'She doesn't show her feelings easily, but that doesn't mean she doesn't have any. I think she had strong feelings for Forley, though there were obviously problems with their relationship.'

'She didn't say much about Catherine Crowther, did she?' said Bowen. 'I'd love to know what the two women really feel about each other.'

Forley's house looked even more lovely in daylight. Its size and shape were perfect, and the sunlight gave an extra richness to the colour of its old walls. Although it was

November, the roses were still beautiful. It seemed impossible that something terrible had happened here the day before.

The telephone was on an antique table next to the wooden stairs in the hall. There were three messages on the answerphone, two from the day before. Amanda Grant had called at 3.45 saying she was back. A few minutes later someone called Philip had invited Forley and Amanda to Sunday lunch. Then at eight o'clock that morning Amanda Grant had phoned again.

'Philip was the name of that doctor Amanda Grant told us about,' remembered Eliot. 'I wonder if it's the same person.'

It was almost half past one when Bowen and Eliot finished searching the house. Forley had obviously been a very tidy man, and everything seemed to be still in its place. They took away a diary, an address book and £2,200 in cash, which was sitting on top of his desk.

'No-one tried to steal his money,' said Bowen. 'So that's not why he was killed. How can people keep so much cash at home? It's just an invitation to criminals.'

'Oh, he probably thought Blackheath was safe,' Eliot answered. 'Remember what Crowther said? People like that don't believe crime will ever happen to them. We'd better go and see them now. I want to know more about that gun she mentioned.'

But the Crowthers were not at home, so Eliot and Bowen decided to have lunch in an old pub on the edge of Blackheath. Through the window they could see the workmen preparing the evening's firework show.

The bonfire was much bigger now. Groups of people

stood looking at the model of Guy Fawkes lying next to it. To Eliot it seemed almost alive with its black hair and beard and seventeenth century hat and coat.

Tonight, many people would watch it burning on top of the bonfire. But few would think about the real Guy Fawkes, who was burned for trying to blow up the Houses of Parliament. His reason had been religious. But most of the people watching tonight would have very little interest in religion. Was anything so important these days that people would kill to protect it? Eliot saw Micky's and Sally's faces in his mind's eye.

He remembered he had to ring them, but the only phone was in the noisiest part of the bar. He sighed. The call would have to wait, but he would look at house prices straight after lunch.

Chapter 9 *Secrets and lies*

Bowen had to ring the bell twice before Catherine Crowther opened the door. Eliot was surprised once again by how lovely she was. She was wearing a green pullover that matched her eyes. And her beauty was strengthened by the unhappiness that showed in her face.

Ronald Crowther was in the sitting room reading a newspaper. He looked up when they walked in, but not before Eliot noticed that his eyes were staring at the top of the front page. He had obviously just picked it up.

He seemed angry and his wife looked very nervous, though they both tried to hide it. They had probably been arguing before the doorbell rang. Eliot decided to question them in different rooms. It would be interesting to see if their stories were the same.

'We'd like to ask you both a few more questions,' he said. 'Mrs Crowther, could you show me where you were painting yesterday? Detective Constable Bowen will speak to Mr Crowther down here.'

He knew that Bowen would have preferred to speak to Catherine Crowther, but the younger man did not let any disappointment show on his face. He got out his notebook as Catherine Crowther led Eliot away.

She took him upstairs to a room with white walls and no furniture, which smelled pleasantly of paint. Eliot could see the backs of several paintings standing against the walls, and another by the window which was not quite finished.

The colours were surprising. Unlike the blues and greens of the pictures downstairs, this painting was in black, dark red and orange. It contained a lot of violence. Eliot could hardly believe it had been painted by the same person.

'What made her change to this style of painting?' he wondered. 'And when did it happen? I'd love to know what the paintings over there are like.'

He looked through the window, and had a perfect view of PC Drewitt standing outside Forley's front door with a cigarette in his hand.

If Catherine Crowther spent a lot of time painting up here, she would know all about Forley's private life.

'How long were you up here yesterday?' he asked.

'Most of the morning,' she said. 'I suppose I started painting at about half past nine. I stopped at about twelve o'clock, and began again just after three, as I told you yesterday. But I didn't see any visitors in the afternoon.'

'What about the morning?' asked Eliot.

'Well, someone did come just before I stopped,' she said. 'But I didn't see his face. I only looked up as he was going through the front door.'

'So you have no idea who he was?' Eliot asked.

'Well.' She stopped for a moment. 'From behind he looked a bit like Philip Wilver. He's a friend of Alex's, and his doctor. The man had the same colour hair, and a navy-blue jacket like Philip. But I can't be sure it was him, Inspector. I only saw him for a second.'

'That's very helpful,' said Eliot. 'Do you think your husband saw him?'

'Ronald was working in the back garden all morning,' she said. 'He wouldn't have seen anything. I suppose he might have heard something if they'd gone out into Alex's garden, though. You'd better ask him.'

'We will,' replied Eliot. 'Now, we need to know more about Mr Forley. What kind of man was he?'

She looked into the distance and her eyes filled with tears.

'A very interesting man,' she said. 'And a very kind one. Sometimes too kind. He hated hurting people, and it made him rather weak.'

She seemed to be sorry she had said this, and went on very quickly, 'It's impossible to believe that anyone would want to hurt him.'

'You said yesterday that you didn't believe it was suicide,' said Eliot. 'What made you so sure?'

She looked away quickly. 'I didn't know what I was saying yesterday, Inspector. Of course it's possible that he killed himself. Anyone could commit suicide if the situation was difficult enough.'

'And was Mr Forley in a difficult situation?' asked Eliot with interest. Until now he had believed that Alex's life had been easy. Too easy, if Amanda was right.

'Well, I could see he had something on his mind that he wouldn't talk about,' she said. 'But he usually told me everything. He didn't keep secrets.'

'She's talking about him like a lover,' thought Eliot.

'Don't misunderstand me, Inspector,' she said quickly. 'Alex and I were very close. He was probably my best friend, but we didn't have a love affair. My husband had no worries about our relationship. He knew everything that happened between us.'

'I see,' said Eliot, not believing this at all. 'Now, you

mentioned a gun last night. Can you tell me more about it?'

'Did I?' she said, looking away. 'I was so shocked yesterday. I've forgotten what I said. But I do remember Ronald and Alex joking about one recently. It was after Alex had bought a valuable painting for his house. Ronald asked if he had ever thought about being robbed, and Alex said he'd better go out and buy a gun. Maybe that's what I was thinking about last night. But neither of them were serious, Inspector. Nothing ever happens in Blackheath.'

She looked as if she knew Eliot did not believe her. She was not a very good liar.

'Now, I understand Mr Forley had been worried about his health,' he went on. 'Could you tell me about it?'

'Oh, yes,' she said quickly, as if pleased to change the subject. 'He'd had a lot of headaches, and he took them very seriously. That was how his mother's illness started, Inspector. She died of a brain tumour, you see, and it wasn't pleasant. Alex was getting really worried.'

'And would you say that Mr Forley was a lazy man?' asked Eliot, remembering what Amanda Grant had said.

'Not at all, Inspector,' she answered. 'He didn't spend all his time doing business, if that's what you mean. But there are many other kinds of work. Alex loved music and books and paintings, and he gave a lot of time to them. Of course, some people would not consider that work, because it doesn't make any money.'

She looked at Eliot as if she was wondering whether he belonged to this group of people.

'What was his relationship with Miss Grant like?' he asked. 'Do you think they were happy together.'

She was quiet for a moment. Then she said, 'Amanda is a young woman of the world, Inspector. She wants to be successful and she couldn't see that Alex's values were different. She didn't always understand him. It caused problems between them.'

'What kind of problems?' asked Eliot.

'Alex wanted to marry her, but she couldn't make up her mind. She wanted him to take more interest in his business. It made Alex very unhappy.'

She looked at Eliot sadly for a moment.

'She didn't realise how lucky she was,' she said. 'And now it's too late. Too late to change anything.'

She put her hand over her eyes to hide her tears.

Chapter 10   *Falling in love again*

Unlike many men, Eliot did not feel uncomfortable when women cried. In his job he was quite used to it. He watched Mrs Crowther closely, but without appearing to. She was clearly unhappy, but it was also obvious that she was hiding something. Maybe it had nothing to do with Forley's death. And maybe Forley's death was suicide. But still he wanted to know what it was.

For the moment, though, he could ask only routine questions.

'There's one more thing that interests me,' he said. 'We've found a lot of money in Mr Forley's house. Did he always keep large amounts of cash at home?'

'I have no idea, Inspector,' she said in surprise. 'Money isn't something I usually discuss.'

'No,' thought Eliot. 'I suppose you don't need to when you've got so much.'

They went out of the door. Eliot stopped in front of a painting outside the room. It was similar to the ones downstairs.

'May I ask if this is one of yours?' he said.

She nodded, looking surprised again, and he went on, 'It's very different from the one you're working on now.'

'Oh, I wanted to try something new,' she said lightly. She turned quickly towards the stairs, but not before Eliot had seen her face was starting to burn.

Bowen and Ronald Crowther were waiting for them in the hall.

'If there's anything more we can tell you, please ask,' said Ronald Crowther. 'Alex was a wonderful man. We want to do everything we can to help.'

'Oh there is one thing. I understand you were working outside yesterday morning, sir,' said Eliot. 'Did you hear anything from Forley's garden?'

'Not a thing, I'm afraid, Inspector,' said Ronald Crowther.

He opened the door to let them out, and stood looking at them as they walked down the path towards the gate.

In the car they compared the Crowthers' stories, which seemed to agree in every detail.

'What about that story of the gun, sir?' asked Bowen. 'Do you believe it?'

'Not a word of it,' Eliot said. 'They're obviously lying. I wonder why. What did you think of Ronald Crowther?'

'Well, he's not as intelligent as his wife,' answered Bowen. 'And he's obviously unhappy about Forley, but not as unhappy as she is. I'd say he's worried about something, frightened maybe.'

'I think it would take a lot to frighten a man like Crowther,' said Eliot. 'He doesn't seem to be a man of very much imagination.'

'From what you've said, sir, Catherine Crowther didn't have a very high opinion of Amanda Grant.'

'No, she seemed to feel she understood Forley better than Amanda.'

'Do you think Forley and Catherine Crowther were having an affair, sir?'

'I don't know,' Eliot said. 'She was obviously very close to him because he told her why he was so worried about his headaches. Even Amanda didn't seem to know that.'

'So what's our next move?' asked Bowen.

'Well, we can't question them again before we've seen the pathologist's report on Monday,' said Eliot. 'But we'll go and see Philip Wilver first thing tomorrow. I wonder if he was the man that Catherine Crowther saw yesterday. His name keeps appearing everywhere. He may have something to tell us.'

They decided to call in at Forley's shop in Greenwich, and as they turned into Park Street they saw streams of tourists walking towards the river. Many were eating ice creams, although it was now quite cold and already starting to get dark.

It was a long street of tall smart houses. Their windows and doors were all the same dark blue, but plants grew everywhere, in front gardens and window boxes, giving it colour and life. There were only two shops, which both sold antiques. They stood side by side, as if they needed each other's company among the houses all around. Above the door of the larger one was Forley's name in gold letters.

The windows held almost nothing. In one there was a small table with a beautiful metal lamp on it. In the other a large Chinese pot stood on a richly coloured Persian carpet.

Eliot must have been mad to imagine he could afford anything here. And the house prices he had seen had amazed him. But he would find the money sooner or later, even if he had to work every weekend for a year.

Although it was only four o'clock, a sign on the door said 'Closed'. But a young woman was sitting at a table inside. He knocked once on the door, and then again, more loudly, when she did not move. He held up his policeman's card, and she came quickly to the door. It was obvious she had been crying.

'I'm Linda Scott,' she said. 'I'm the manager here. I suppose you've come about poor Alex. He was such a lovely man. Of course, I closed the shop immediately when Amanda phoned. Do you have any idea how it happened?'

Eliot was glad she already knew. He did not like giving bad news. He had already had to tell enough people about Forley's death.

'I'm afraid it's still too early to say,' he said. 'But you might be able to help us. Did you see Mr Forley yesterday?'

'Yes. He always came on Fridays,' she said. 'He was here from about nine-thirty to eleven.'

'And did he do anything unusual?' asked Bowen.

'No, I don't think so,' she said. 'He made a few phone calls and wrote some letters. He did take quite a lot of money away but that wasn't unusual. He said he was planning to buy something. In this business people often prefer to be paid in cash. It stops them having to pay tax.'

She stopped and looked worried. She suddenly seemed to remember she was talking to a policeman.

Bowen smiled at her, though he didn't usually find it funny when people talked about breaking the law.

'Do you know how much money he took?' asked Bowen, still smiling.

'Just over £2,000, I think,' she said, opening a large notebook. 'Yes, £2,200.'

'Just one more thing before we go,' said Eliot. 'Was Mr Forley a good employer?'

'Wonderful,' she said. 'He was kind and human. So different from most employers these days. But recently he'd been looking unhappy. He seemed worried about something. He said he'd been getting headaches, but it must have been more than that.'

Bowen wrote down her address before they left the shop.

'Why was Forley so attractive to women?' he asked Eliot in the car. 'None of them have a bad word to say about him. She seems to have been half in love with him herself.'

'But it didn't do him much good, did it?' said Eliot. 'What's the matter, Bowen? Are you getting jealous of him?'

He had been joking. But a look at Bowen's face showed him the other man was quite serious.

'Just don't get any ideas about Linda Scott until the case is over,' Eliot warned.

'No, sir,' said Bowen.

'You'll have to keep an open mind about her,' continued Eliot. 'She may be guilty of his murder.'

He had no real reason for thinking this. And he had to admit that she seemed nicer than the girls Bowen usually liked. But with Bowen's luck, nothing would surprise him.

Chapter 11 *Homes and families*

At last he was home. Eliot took off his tie, poured himself a beer and rang Sally's parents' number. He half expected no-one to be at home, but Sally picked up the phone before the second ring. She sounded pleased to hear his voice.

'Hello Rod,' she said. 'Where have you been all day? I rang the station four times.'

'Blackheath and Greenwich mostly,' he replied. 'I've got a new murder, but I'm not getting very far with it. There's a dead man who everybody loved. And a lot of money in his house, but none of it stolen. It might have been suicide, but we won't know till Monday. Are you all right?'

'Yes, we've had a lovely day,' she said. 'It's a pity you had to stay in London. But you sound happier than you were on Friday.'

'Yes, I'm sorry I was in such a terrible mood,' Eliot said. 'How's Micky?'

'Having a great time. But he's missing you a lot. He can't stop talking about you. You'd better have a word with him.'

'Hello, Dad,' said Micky.

Eliot smiled as his son talked about the beach and tonight's firework show. He always got so much pleasure from life. Eliot was sorry not to be with him.

But when he put the phone down, he realised he felt tired. The thought of a quiet evening in front of the television suddenly seemed very pleasant. *Match of the Day* would be enough excitement for this evening, if he could keep awake long enough to watch it.

He was pleased that Sally was not angry with him. In fact, she was never angry for long. But it did not stop Eliot feeling uncomfortable after arguments. There could always be a first time.

He made himself some food, went into the sitting room and turned on the news. The government was in trouble again. Eliot tried to listen to the details through the sounds of fireworks exploding outside. But he was too tired to be very interested.

He fell asleep in the middle of the Saturday night hospital drama. But the shouting of football fans woke him up after two hours. West Ham had just scored the winning goal, three minutes from the end. Eliot smiled as he turned off the television.

Next morning the weather had changed. It was the first day of winter.

When he arrived at the office, Bowen was already there. Eliot thought he had not looked so happy for months.

'Morning, Bowen. Did you have a good evening?' he asked.

'Well, I thought Forley's diary might help us, sir,' he said. 'So I took it home to look at. He obviously didn't want anyone else to understand it. It's written in Greek and Latin mixed together, but I think I'm just beginning to see how it works. It will take a bit of time, though, before I can read it.'

'Education is a wonderful thing,' said Eliot. But he himself had joined the police as soon as he left school. And he did not think a university education would have helped him very much. Reading had never been important to him. He preferred learning from experience.

But he was pleased with the younger man. Bowen was always a fast worker, and now he had an extra interest in the case. The sooner they finished it, the sooner he could try his luck with Linda Scott. Eliot hoped his feelings for her would not affect his judgement.

'Well, we'd better go and see Philip Wilver,' said Eliot. 'Let's hope he's at home.'

'Most people are on Sunday morning,' said Bowen. 'Except policemen.'

Pepys Road was a beautiful street very near Eliot's own house. The houses were large, with big rooms and high ceilings. Many had been separated into flats, but Number 54 was still a single house. Eliot had sometimes looked in through the lighted windows on winter evenings. It always looked inviting with its beautiful fireplace and the large mirror on the wall above it.

Eliot was sad to see the roses in the front garden were turning brown, probably because of last night's cold weather, he thought. They would soon be dead. He knew he would find the same in his own garden, when he had time to look.

Bowen rang the doorbell while Eliot looked through the window, blowing on his hands to keep them warm. A man and a young boy were sitting together on a sofa. They were looking at a picture book. Eliot was disappointed to see that no-one had lit the fire.

The door was opened by a tall dark-haired woman with a cigarette in her hand. She looked pale and stressed. She stared at them for a few seconds without speaking. It was as if she didn't see them.

'Yes?' she said eventually.

'We'd like to speak to Philip Wilver,' said Eliot after he had introduced them. 'Is he at home?'

She went inside and called, 'Philip! It's the police.'

A few seconds later, the man from the sofa appeared. He was tall and good-looking with short dark hair and glasses. He looked nervous, like his wife, but seemed more in control. The young boy was with him, holding on to his leg and staring at the policemen with wide eyes. Eliot thought he must be about five years old.

'I'm Philip Wilver,' said the man. 'I'm sorry my wife kept you waiting outside. Please come in.'

They went into the room Eliot had seen from the outside. It was surprisingly untidy. Papers and magazines lay on the floor next to unwashed cups and ashtrays full of cigarette ends. But this did not hide the fact that it was a beautiful room.

'I'm sorry about the mess,' said Wilver. 'Some friends came over yesterday morning and gave us some terrible news. A friend of ours has died suddenly.'

He looked at them sadly.

'I suppose that's why you've come,' he said.

'I'm afraid so, sir,' said Eliot.

Wilver put his hand on the boy's shoulder.

'Go and find your mother, Sam,' he said. 'She's in the back room.'

The child got up slowly and went out. He did not say a word.

'He's very unhappy about Alex,' said his father. 'Alex was

very good with kids. Sam really loved him. Have you found out what happened to him, Inspector?'

'Not yet, sir,' said Eliot. 'But we're hoping you may be able to help us. We understand you knew him quite well. You were also his doctor, weren't you?'

'Only for a few months, Inspector,' said Wilver. 'I knew him better as a friend.'

'We've heard he was ill,' said Eliot. 'Is this true?'

'Not really,' replied Wilver. 'Though for a time he thought he was. He'd been having a lot of headaches and thought they might be serious. But I knew they weren't. He even persuaded me to arrange some tests at Guy's Hospital. A complete waste of money. But that was all I could do to stop him worrying.'

'When are you expecting the results?' asked Eliot.

'Oh, they arrived this week. Of course they showed nothing. He probably just needed a new pair of glasses.'

He turned away again. 'Poor Alex,' he said.

Chapter 12 *One kind of marriage*

No-one spoke for a few seconds. From the next room they could hear Wilver's wife talking to the child. She sounded angry. The boy did not seem to be saying anything.

'Excuse me, Inspector,' said Wilver. 'I'd better get Sam. Lisa's finding him rather difficult at the moment. She's been badly affected by Alex's death. We all have.'

He went out for a moment, and reappeared carrying his son. The boy was crying, his head pressed against his father's shoulder.

'It's all right, Sam,' said Wilver gently. 'Mummy's just a bit busy at the moment.'

'She's always busy,' Sam said. 'She never plays with me.'

'I'll take you to the park soon,' said his father. 'We'll have a game of football. But I must speak to these people first. Go upstairs and get ready, Sam. I think I saw the football in your bedroom this morning.'

The boy stopped crying and went to the door.

'We'll be as quick as we can, sir,' said Eliot. 'Now, how long had you known Mr Forley?'

'Since university,' said Wilver. 'We met on our first day and found we had a lot in common. Both of us had a parent who died when we were very young. It seemed to bring us together. And when I met Lisa, she liked him too. That was very important. Are you married, Inspector?'

Eliot said he was.

'So you'll understand what it's like,' Wilver continued.

50

'Alex came from a rich family, like Lisa, and that was important to her. She didn't seem to like my other friends, and eventually I stopped seeing them. Lisa was very unhappy when I started my medical studies. I had to work very hard, and she didn't see much of me. I couldn't expect her to spend time with people she didn't like. You know how it is, Inspector.'

'Of course,' said Eliot. But really he did not understand that kind of relationship. Sally and he had always accepted each other's friends.

'And when did you last see Mr Forley?' he asked.

'Friday,' said Wilver. 'When I phoned to give him his test results, he asked me to come round the next day. He said he wanted my advice about something. So I went to his house at about twelve o'clock. But when I got there, he'd changed his mind. He said it wasn't important any more, though he seemed a bit worried about something. I only stayed for a quick cup of coffee. Then I went back to the surgery for my lunchtime meeting.'

'Do you remember what time you left, sir?' asked Bowen.

'Around twenty past twelve,' said Wilver. 'But I couldn't help worrying about him after that. I phoned later to ask him to lunch today, but he wasn't there. I left a message on his answerphone. I expect you've heard it.'

His face changed.

'Was he already dead by then, Inspector?' he asked.

'I'm afraid we don't yet know,' Eliot replied. 'Dr Wilver, was Mr Forley drinking wine when you were there?'

'Wine?' asked Wilver. 'No. Alex didn't drink very much. And he certainly never drank by himself.'

51

'Thank you, sir,' said Eliot. 'Now, there's just one more thing I'd like to ask. What kind of person was Mr Forley?'

Wilver looked at him for a moment.

'It's difficult to describe someone you know well,' he said. 'But I'll try. He was easy to talk to. You could tell him anything, and he'd always say the right thing. He was often serious, but he could be very funny, too. I'm going to miss him a lot.'

'And would you say he was a weak man, sir?' asked Eliot, remembering what Catherine Crowther had said.

The doctor did not answer immediately. He looked at the fireplace and seemed deep in thought for a moment.

'No more than the rest of us, Inspector,' he said at last.

He suddenly made himself smile as Sam came into the room, holding a football. The boy looked at Eliot and sat down on the carpet.

Just before they left, Eliot asked, 'By the way, sir. Can you think of anyone who might have wanted to hurt Mr Forley?'

'No,' said Wilver. 'Everyone loved Alex.'

He closed the front door. Through the window, Eliot saw Sam sitting on the floor, patiently waiting for his father. He could not remember Micky ever sitting so still at that age. For a moment he felt worried about the child. What kind of family life did he have?

'What did you think of him?' asked Eliot as soon as they were in the car.

'Well, he obviously loves his son,' said Bowen. 'But I wouldn't like to be in his shoes. Not with a wife like that. She's good-looking enough, but she obviously rules his life. And she doesn't seem to have much time for the kid.'

'But he must be stronger than he looks,' Eliot said. 'His wife couldn't stop him becoming a doctor. And it can't be easy being married while you're training. Of course, you can see why she wouldn't like it. Not just for the long hours. She's too interested in money, and new doctors don't earn very much.'

He looked at Bowen for a moment.

'This should be a lesson for you,' he said. 'Be careful with the women you choose. And if they don't make you happy, get rid of them.'

Bowen looked embarrassed, and Eliot changed the subject.

'Forley was certainly popular,' he said. 'And not only with women. But I'd love to know what Wilver was thinking about when I asked if he was weak.'

'Yes,' said Bowen. 'He's hiding something from us too.'

'Well, at least we now know it was Wilver who visited Forley on Friday,' said Eliot. 'And we know that Forley wasn't really ill. That takes away one possible reason for suicide. So what else was he worried about?'

'And why was he drinking if he never drank alone?' Bowen asked. 'Maybe someone came to see him after Wilver had left. Someone who was going to sell him something, perhaps. That could be why he had all that money in the house. Maybe that person murdered him, and then washed the second wine glass.'

'It's possible,' said Eliot. 'But who wanted to murder him? Everyone seemed to like him so much. We'll have to talk to the neighbours again and see if anyone saw anything. Can you arrange that? And you'd better take Amanda Grant to look at his house. It didn't look as if anything was missing, but we ought to be sure. I've got a feeling that this case isn't going to be as easy as I first thought.'

Chapter 13 *Home at last*

Eliot sat at his computer and looked at a report he had started on Friday. But questions about the Forley case filled his mind, and he could not push them away.

Why were the Crowthers not telling him the truth? Had Catherine Crowther been having an affair with Forley? What had made her suddenly change her style of painting? And did anyone visit Forley after Wilver had left on Friday? Catherine Crowther would not have seen if they had arrived after one o'clock and gone out through the back gate. And what had Forley been so worried about?

Eliot made a great effort to work. He had three other reports to write, and they should all have been finished days ago. But he could not stop thinking about the case. By the time he went home, he had hardly written anything.

'Dad!' said Micky as soon as he got through the door. 'Did you see that brilliant goal last night?'

'On *Match of the Day*?' Eliot asked. 'Weren't you in bed by then?'

'Mum said I could stay up and watch it,' Micky said.

'He could hardly keep his eyes open,' said Sally.

'Neither could I,' said Eliot. He gave them both a kiss.

Sally had already started the evening meal. Eliot rarely cooked, except for Sunday lunch and on Wednesdays when Sally worked late. She taught part-time at Lewisham College. Her classes were usually over in time to pick up

Micky from school at 3.30, and on other days her sister took care of him.

As soon as he sat down at the kitchen table, he relaxed. Forley's death was a problem which interested him, but did not worry him any more. Forley had had no children or family of his own. Of course, his friends would miss him, but they had their own lives. And Amanda Grant was strong enough to start again. It was not Eliot's business if the Crowthers and the Wilvers had problems with their marriages. He hoped the pathologist would say it was suicide, and that would be the end of it.

But Eliot's feelings told him it was more complicated than suicide. And after eighteen years with the police, he trusted his feelings. He knew that two people were lying, and maybe more. What were they trying to protect?

Still, it could all wait until tomorrow. Now it was time for him to listen to Micky. He smiled as his son began to tell him about last night's firework show.

Chapter 14 *But was it murder?*

Eliot usually found Monday mornings especially unpleasant when he had been working all weekend. But today he woke up in a good mood, which continued until he got to the police station.

Once again, Bowen had arrived before him. He said he had already been there for half an hour.

'What's happened to you?' asked Eliot. 'Last week you could hardly get here on time. It must be love.'

Bowen wished Eliot would stop mentioning his private life.

'I'm just interested in the case,' Bowen answered uncomfortably. 'And there'll be a lot to do today. By the way, Amanda Grant couldn't find anything missing from Forley's house.'

'As I expected,' said Eliot. 'Have we got any of the reports yet?'

'Yes, sir. The pathologist's has just arrived,' answered Bowen. 'It seems they start work early there. And we've got a report on the gun. It's an army gun from the Second World War. They're not very common now. It's almost a collector's piece. There's no record of it anywhere, of course.'

'That's a pity,' said Eliot. 'There won't be much chance of finding where it came from. It's probably been hiding in someone's garage for years.'

Eliot got a cup of coffee from the machine, and sat down to read the pathologist's report.

'Let's hope this tells us something more useful,' he said. 'Did he kill himself or not? That's what we need to know.'

But his hopes were disappointed. The report said that the dead man had been killed by a shot to the head, fired either by himself or another person, between 3.15 and 3.45 in the afternoon. At the time of death, the gun was touching his forehead and he had died immediately. There were no other signs of violence. He had been in very good health, but there was a lot of alcohol in his stomach and blood.

'Well, it doesn't look as if it was an accident,' said Eliot. 'A man would not sit down in a comfortable chair and put a gun to his head unless he meant to kill himself. But who fired the shot? What do you think, Bowen? Was it murder or suicide?'

'Too many people are hiding things from us,' said Bowen. 'I don't believe it was simple suicide. Though someone obviously wanted us to think it was.'

'Is suicide ever simple?' asked Eliot. 'But I think you're right. Now, we know more or less when he died. And the noise that Catherine Crowther heard at half past three was probably the gunshot. That's if she was telling the truth. Find out who's got an alibi for that time, Bowen. And we'll have to get fingerprints. We'll need to see if any of them match the ones we found in Forley's house.'

'Yes, sir,' said Bowen. 'And Forley seems to have drunk quite a lot. Much more than one glass of wine.'

'So maybe you were right, Bowen,' said Eliot. 'Maybe

Forley did invite someone to lunch that day. What did the neighbours say?'

'Nothing important. No-one saw anything.'

'Or maybe Forley drank to make it easier to kill himself,' continued Eliot thoughtfully. 'Everyone keeps saying he was worried about something. Have you found anything useful in his diary?'

'Not yet,' said Bowen. 'It's slow work. It's a long time since I read any Latin or Greek. But I'll keep trying.'

Eliot sat down at his desk. Yesterday's work stared up at him. He hoped he would be able to finish all his reports before Bowen got back. He sighed. Detectives had to do a lot of writing these days. The job had not always been like this.

Eliot worked through the lunch hour, and he managed to finish the last report just after half past two. He put his coat on, and went across the road to The Queen's Head. The barman started pouring him a beer as soon as he walked through the door.

The pub was empty now except for a noisy group of students at one end of the bar. They had all finished their drinks but they did not seem to be in any hurry to leave.

Eliot sat down by the window, as far away as possible. The beer tasted good. He opened his newspaper and turned to the sports page. He decided to give himself half an hour's break. He had certainly earned it after all that writing.

But he had only just started the report on Saturday's West Ham match when Bowen walked through the door. Eliot sighed. But the news Bowen gave him took all thoughts of football from his mind.

Chapter 15   *Uncovering lies*

'Sorry, sir,' said Bowen. 'But I thought you'd want to hear this as soon as possible. It seems that Forley had a cleaning lady, a Mrs Brook. She went to his house this morning, and got angry when they wouldn't let her in. Mondays and Thursdays were the days she worked for him. And she worked for the Crowthers on Wednesdays.

'Anyway, she's given us some very interesting information. It seems that Forley went to see Catherine Crowther on Wednesday afternoon, when Ronald was out.'

'That *is* interesting,' said Eliot. 'Mrs Crowther told us she hadn't seen him for a week. What did Mrs Brook say about the visit?'

'Apparently, Forley was there for about an hour,' Bowen replied. 'The sitting room door was closed, so she couldn't hear anything. But when they came out, Mrs Crowther was as white as a sheet, and Forley looked very uncomfortable.'

'I wonder what Catherine Crowther will have to say about that,' said Eliot.

'But that's not all, sir,' continued Bowen. 'Mrs Brook said that Crowther had an old gun. Apparently, it had belonged to his father. She came into the room once when he was cleaning it. He quickly put it back into a drawer in his desk, but not before she had seen it. She said she could never go into the sitting room again without wondering if it was still there.'

'He kept it in a desk?' said Eliot. 'That was stupid. And I

don't suppose he had a licence for it. Well, that gives us something to think about. What about the fingerprints? Have you had any luck with them?'

'Well, sir,' said Bowen. 'There were four sets of fresh fingerprints found in the house besides Forley's.'

'So, all we have to do is find out whose fingerprints they are. Our suspects are the Crowthers, the Wilvers, Amanda Grant and Mrs Brook. Can we be sure about what any of them were doing on Friday afternoon?'

'Well, we know Mrs Brook spent the day with her sister. And Wilver was in the surgery from twelve forty-five to six o'clock,' said Bowen. 'He had two meetings, and then he saw patients. He didn't have a free moment. And his wife was having lunch with a friend in Greenwich. She left at three-fifteen to pick up her son from school.'

'What about the other three?' asked Eliot.

'We haven't been able to check their stories,' said Bowen. 'Catherine Crowther was alone at home. Ronald was out walking, but he doesn't remember seeing anybody. And Amanda Grant went straight to her house when she got back.

'But there's something else, sir,' he continued. 'I looked at a few more pages of Forley's diary while I was waiting at the surgery, and I found something very interesting. It seems Alex Forley wasn't the golden boy everybody thinks he was. He was having a secret love affair.'

'With Catherine Crowther?' asked Eliot.

'I'm afraid I can't tell you that,' said Bowen. 'He changed everyone's names.'

'Well, I think we'd better go and have a look at Ronald's gun, don't you?' said Eliot.

He stood up, leaving his beer half drunk. The students were still sitting at the other end of the bar. They would probably stay all afternoon if the barman let them. It was much warmer in the pub than in the rooms which they rented.

Eliot felt some excitement as he rang the Crowthers' bell. The pieces seemed to be coming together. With any luck the case would be over by the evening.

But neither of the Crowthers were at home.

'I suppose he's gone for his usual walk,' said Eliot. 'But I wonder where she can be. I thought she'd be painting in her room.'

He looked up at the window. Was it his imagination, or did he see someone moving quickly away from the window? He rang the bell again, this time for at least five seconds. But again there was no reply.

'Let's wait in that pub where we went on Saturday,' he said. 'At least it's warm in there, and I can have the second half of my lunch.'

Today the pub was much less crowded, and they easily found a seat. Eliot looked outside, and at first forgot that Saturday had been Guy Fawkes Night. There was no fence and there were no fireworks. People were walking about as usual, and the only sign of the bonfire was a dark shape on the ground.

Suddenly, he saw a tall man in a dark coat on the other side of the grass. Eliot thought he recognised him.

'I think that's Ronald Crowther,' he said. 'Don't you, Bowen?'

But the barman, who was bringing Eliot a sandwich, answered instead.

'Yes, that's Mr Crowther, sir,' he said. 'He's always here at this time, in rain or sunshine. He comes at three o'clock and goes at four. Regular as a clock. Most people would find it boring walking up and down the same piece of grass, never talking to anyone. But he doesn't seem to mind. People are strange.'

'I don't suppose you noticed him here on Friday,' said Eliot.

'Friday?' the barman said. 'Of course I did. I see him every day. At first I thought he was late, but it was my watch that was fast. Like I said, you can tell the time from his coming and going.'

As Eliot finished his sandwich, he saw Crowther turn back to his house. He checked his watch. Exactly four o'clock. The barman had been telling the truth. So Crowther had been out for a walk when Forley died.

But the policemen followed him back to his house anyway. Ronald Crowther could not be the murderer, but he and his wife still had a lot of questions to answer.

Chapter 16 *Jealousy*

Eliot did not return the Crowthers' smiles when they opened the door. He knew they were not at all pleased to see him. Their politeness and gentleness were just a cover. They had been playing games with him from the beginning.

Without any introduction, he asked if Crowther had a gun. The man's face went white, and his wife sat down quickly, as if her legs had lost all their strength.

'And I'd like the truth this time,' said Eliot. 'We've wasted enough time already.'

'Yes, Inspector,' said Crowther. 'I've had a gun for years. It belonged to my father. He kept it to remember the war, and he also kept one bullet. When he died, I kept it to remember him. I suppose that was a stupid thing to do.'

'It was a crime if you had no licence for it,' said Eliot. 'May I see it, please?'

Ronald Crowther covered his face with his hands.

'I haven't got it, Inspector. Alex took it about three weeks ago. We were having friends to dinner, and someone started discussing the war. I'd drunk rather a lot, and stupidly told them about it. Alex loved old things, and of course he wanted to see it.

'Then he said it might be worth a lot of money. He asked if he could borrow it to have it valued. I couldn't see any harm in it, so I gave it to him. I told him there was a bullet inside, but he wasn't worried. He said he knew how to use guns. He'd been taught at school.'

Eliot could feel his anger rising inside him. What kind of world did these people think they were living in? Did they think they were above the law?

'And who else was at this dinner party?' asked Eliot.

But he felt he knew the answer before it came. The Crowthers, the Wilvers and Amanda Grant, the tight little circle that had surrounded Forley until he died.

'Why didn't you tell us this before?' he asked.

Ronald Crowther said he wished he had. But then he had suddenly realised that keeping a gun was against the law. He and his wife had decided that the best thing to do was to keep quiet.

'Mr Crowther, we'll have to ask you to come to the police station immediately,' said Eliot. 'We need to know if it was your gun which killed Mr Forley.'

The Crowthers looked at each other. They seemed frightened.

'And Mrs Crowther, could you tell us when you last saw Mr Forley?' Eliot asked.

She lifted her green eyes to his.

'As I told you, Inspector,' she answered, 'it was a week ago on Friday.'

'Could you think very carefully about that?' said Eliot.

'I don't need to,' she said. 'I remember very well.'

'Mrs Crowther,' said Eliot. 'I'll have to ask you to come to the station with us too. We need to question you again about the death of Alex Forley.'

'*Me?*' she said. 'You want to question *me*? But I thought . . .'

She stopped suddenly. Ronald Crowther had closed his eyes. He looked like a man in the middle of a bad dream.

Eliot told Bowen not to leave the couple alone together. He did not want to give them a chance to think of another story.

At the police station, they were taken to separate rooms. They both nodded when Eliot showed them the gun.

Ronald Crowther was looking tired and much older than when Eliot had first seen him, and his wife suddenly seemed middle-aged. Eliot decided to question her first.

'We have spoken to someone who says Mr Forley visited you last Wednesday afternoon,' he said.

'Have you? I suppose it was Mrs Brook,' she answered after a short silence. 'I forgot all about her.'

Perhaps people like Mrs Brook were not important enough for her to remember. Eliot wondered again what sort of person Alex Forley had been. How could a man be so close to two such different women as Catherine Crowther and Amanda Grant?

'Yes, it's true,' Catherine Crowther continued. 'Alex did come to see me then. We discussed something very private. Alex even asked me not to tell Ronald about it.'

'Nothing is private after a violent death,' said Eliot impatiently. 'As you should know very well.'

She was silent for a long time.

'Well, Alex had been having a secret relationship,' she said at last. 'I suppose you'd call it an affair, though he was very unhappy about it. It started one evening after a party, when Amanda was away and he was feeling lonely and unhappy. Of course, he immediately wished it hadn't happened. But the woman said she was in love with him, and he didn't know how to end it without hurting her. She was the wife of a friend of his. That's what made it so awful. And that's why I didn't tell you before.'

'Who was she?' asked Eliot.

'Lisa Wilver,' said Catherine Crowther, looking angry.

'Mrs Crowther, were you in love with Mr Forley?' asked Eliot.

She looked at Eliot for a moment.

'Perhaps I was,' she answered. 'We were so close, but nothing ever happened, Inspector. I would never do anything to hurt Ronald. He has been so good to me.'

'And how did you feel when you heard about this affair?'

'Very angry. You've seen my latest painting, Inspector. But it wasn't just jealousy. I thought Alex was so stupid. Lisa's not a very nice person, though he always believed the best of everybody. Her husband's crazy about her, but she doesn't care about him, or her son. She liked Alex because he had money. She thought she had got him, and she wasn't going to let him go. Alex wasn't strong enough to end it. And then, of course, he got so worried about his health.'

'What did you say to him about the affair?' asked Eliot.

'I told him he should finish it immediately,' she answered. 'I also told him how stupid I thought he had been.'

'And why didn't you tell us before about your last meeting with Mr Forley?'

'Oh, I don't really know, Inspector. It was silly of me.'

She really was not a good liar, Eliot thought again. He felt very impatient. What reason could she have for continuing to lie? He knew about the gun, about Alex's last

67

visit and about his affair. And she'd even admitted her own jealousy. What else could she have to hide?

And then Eliot realised. She must be trying to protect her husband.

'Mrs Crowther,' he said, 'we know that your husband was nowhere near Mr Forley's house when he died.'

She stared at Eliot. She seemed unsure about whether to believe him.

'Somebody saw him when he was out walking,' he continued.

'Oh, thank God,' she said. 'I've been so afraid. I didn't know Ronald could be jealous until recently. But suddenly he started asking questions about my relationship with Alex. He couldn't stop talking about it. Alex hadn't spent much time with him lately because he was too worried about his own problems. But Ronald thought it had something to do with me. I don't know if Ronald was more jealous of Alex or of me, but it was very frightening.

'I didn't really believe he'd killed Alex. But he kept asking if Alex ever came to see me when he was out. I couldn't tell him about Wednesday's visit because Alex had made me promise not to. But I think perhaps Ronald saw him leaving the house. Anyway, Ronald could see I was very unhappy about something.

'I didn't want to make the situation worse by telling you about Alex's visit in front of him. Of course, there was nothing for him to be jealous about. Believe me, Inspector. Nothing ever happened between me and Alex.'

Except, perhaps, in your mind, thought Eliot.

At last, he felt she was telling him the truth. As a strong woman, she was clearly not used to lying. But her guilt about her feelings for Forley had made her very confused. And it had wasted a lot of his time.

He watched Catherine and Ronald Crowther leave the police station together. They had obviously been living in fear for the last few days, each believing the other had killed Forley. He wondered how they would explain this when they got home.

'But if neither of them murdered Alex Forley, how did he die?' thought Eliot. 'At last we know what was worrying him so much recently. But surely his relationship with Lisa Wilver wasn't enough to make him kill himself.

'It's true we've now found two other people who possibly wanted him dead. Philip Wilver, if he knew about his wife's affair. And Lisa Wilver, if Forley had tried to finish it. But both of them were with other people that afternoon. There's no question about that.

'No. If someone had been with Forley on Friday afternoon, there was only one person it could be.'

Chapter 17   *Putting the pieces together*

Amanda Grant looked surprised when she opened the door to Eliot and Bowen. But she calmly asked them to come in. She was wearing the same jeans and sweater as on Saturday morning, and today she seemed more like a teenage girl than a successful journalist.

Eliot felt very disappointed. He had liked her from the moment he had first seen her, and he was not usually so wrong about people. She was certainly a woman of strong character and feelings. And he believed most people could kill if the situation was right. Perhaps she had found out about Forley's affair and been unable to accept it. But he had thought she was a brave person. Why hadn't she admitted the crime immediately, instead of trying to cover it up?

'Miss Grant,' he said, 'we would like to know exactly what you did when you got back from Edinburgh.'

'I told Detective Constable Bowen this morning,' she said, in her deep voice. 'The plane landed at London City Airport at five past two. I picked up my car from the car park, and drove back. It took over an hour. The traffic was terrible that day.'

'I understand nobody saw you,' continued Eliot.

'No,' she answered. 'Is it important?'

'These are just routine questions,' said Eliot. 'Now, what did you do when you got home?'

'I unpacked and had a bath,' she said. 'Then I tried to

phone Alex, as you'll know if you've checked his answerphone.'

'Miss Grant, do you have a mobile phone?' asked Eliot.

'Of course,' she answered. 'But I didn't use it to ring Alex, if that's what you're asking. I used that phone over there.'

Eliot was suddenly very pleased. Her story would be easy to check. The airport car park would be able to tell them when she had left, and the phone company would have a record of her calls. If she had phoned from home, it would not have been possible for her to kill Forley. With all that traffic, she could not have got to his house before 3.20 at the earliest. And she certainly would not have been home again by 3.45. For once, he was thankful for the traffic.

In the car Bowen was silent, and Eliot knew he was angry with himself. He had forgotten to ask her about the mobile phone when he saw her that morning. But it would only have saved a little time. Much less time than they had wasted on the Crowthers.

Back at the station, it took Bowen only twenty minutes to check Amanda's story. Someone from her office in Edinburgh had driven her to the airport, and the plane had arrived at five past two, as she had said. Both the car park and the phone company gave the same information as she had given them.

'So it looks as though she's not guilty either,' said Eliot. 'And she's the one who gets everything he owned. We've just spoken to his lawyer. It seems Forley made a will two weeks ago, and left everything to her. But I'm not sure how pleased she'll be. She didn't seem very comfortable about his money.'

Was this case really as unusual as it seemed? Money or love were at the root of most situations the police had to work with. And there were plenty of both here. He felt they must have something to do with Alex Forley's death. But he could not discover what it was. He was finding more and more people with a reason for killing Forley. But it seemed that none of them had had the opportunity.

Eliot did not believe Lisa Wilver would tell them anything useful when they spoke to her. He was beginning to think that Alex Forley had killed himself after all.

That evening, Eliot was quieter than usual, though he always tried not to bring his work home. It was not fair that his family should suffer because of his job. He made a great effort to listen to one of Micky's long stories about his school friends. But Eliot felt something about the case was wrong. He trusted his feelings, and he did not have much time.

'So then Paul hit David, and Miss Thomas made him sit by himself for half an hour. I'm glad he hit him,' Micky was saying.

'But you shouldn't hit people,' said Eliot automatically.

'Yes, but do you know what David did, Dad? He told Paul Miss Thomas had given us five pages of homework, but she hadn't given us any.'

'Why did he tell a lie like that?' Eliot tried to be interested.

'Paul broke his pen and he was angry with him. Do you know how long Paul took to do his homework? Two and a half hours. And he hates maths. Wasn't David horrible? Dad! What are you doing? Put me down!'

Eliot had suddenly picked up his surprised son and was dancing with him round the kitchen.

'Thanks, Micky,' he said. 'I understand it now. Your story was a great help.'

Eliot had suddenly realised what he had missed. Now he thought he knew what had happened to Forley. But before he could be sure, there was something he needed to check. And he would have to ask Bowen to finish reading Forley's diary.

Chapter 18 *The truth at last*

'But why have you brought me here?' asked Dr Wilver. 'I'm a very busy man.'

Eliot had chosen the biggest and smartest of the interview rooms. It had just been painted and the furniture was new. He wanted Wilver to feel relaxed.

'Oh, we just need a little more information,' said Eliot. 'It's completely routine. And we'd like to record this interview. You don't mind, do you, sir?'

Wilver shook his head and Eliot switched on the cassette machine.

'Now, could you tell us again about your last meeting with Mr Forley?' he asked.

Wilver repeated what he had told them the last time they had seen him. At first he seemed nervous, as if he was waiting for Eliot to speak. But he soon began to relax. Eliot listened carefully and nodded from time to time.

'Thank you, sir,' he said politely, after Wilver had finished. 'And now, would you tell us again where you were on the afternoon when he died? This is just routine, of course. We have to ask everybody.'

Wilver relaxed even more.

'Yes, of course, though I did tell Detective Constable Bowen yesterday. I was in the surgery all afternoon. Plenty of people saw me. I'm surprised you haven't asked them, Inspector. But perhaps you've been busy too.'

He smiled at Eliot. But the smile began to disappear after Eliot's next question.

'Dr Wilver, when did you give Mr Forley his test results?'

'As I told you, I phoned him on Thursday evening. You can check with the phone company.'

'And when did you receive them from the hospital, sir?' asked Eliot.

Dr Wilver looked away.

'Probably on Thursday morning,' he said. 'But it's difficult to remember exactly.'

'Even when the patient is a good friend who is seriously worried about them?' asked Eliot.

'I'm afraid so, Inspector. We get so many test results,' said Wilver.

A line of sweat appeared on his forehead.

'Well, let me help your memory,' he said. 'The hospital phoned to give you the results on Monday morning. Now, could you tell us why you waited so long to pass them on to Mr Forley?'

The doctor dried his forehead with a handkerchief.

'It just escaped my memory,' he said. 'I was very busy all last week.'

'But not too busy to go and see Mr Forley on Friday. No, I don't believe that. I think you had a very good reason for keeping the results secret, Dr Wilver.'

'What can you possibly mean?' asked the doctor.

'I think you know what I mean,' said Eliot. 'When you phoned Mr Forley on Thursday, I don't think you gave him his test results. I think you told him you needed some money and wanted to sell something. That's why he took so much cash home. Then when you went to see him on Friday, you lied about his results. You told him he had a brain tumour. You knew that he was planning to kill himself if the test showed he had one. He'd discussed it with you. And you knew he had Crowther's gun.'

'I don't know what you're talking about,' said Wilver. 'Alex never discussed killing himself with me. If he had, I would have told him not to. I'm a doctor, and I was his friend. What reason would I have had? You've been watching too much television, Inspector.'

'The reason was your wife, Lisa,' said Eliot. 'You knew she was having an affair with Mr Forley. And you knew she wanted to leave you for him. You couldn't allow that, could you, sir? We have Mr Forley's diary. We know all about the affair, and we know he told you about his plans to kill himself.'

At the mention of the diary, all the blood seemed to leave Wilver's face. He put his head in his hands. There was a long silence. When he started to speak, Eliot and Bowen had to move forward to hear what he was saying.

'Alex never had to fight for anything,' he said. 'He had everything he wanted. But he couldn't take Lisa away. I wouldn't let Sam grow up without a mother, as I had to. I've worked so hard for what I've got. I wouldn't let anyone take it away from me. You were right, Inspector. Alex was weak. I knew he couldn't live with a brain tumour. So I made him think he might have one. He didn't realise it was my suggestion. I even persuaded him to clean the gun so there were no fingerprints on it. It was so easy. Much too easy.'

He looked at Eliot for a moment.

'The funny thing is that Lisa's left me anyway,' he said with a sound that was almost like a laugh.

'What did you tell him you wanted to sell, Doctor?' Eliot asked quietly.

'The mirror in my sitting room. It's the nicest thing I own.'

He looked at Eliot for a moment.

'I didn't think you'd realise, Inspector,' he said with a small smile. 'You didn't seem especially intelligent.'

Eliot did not reply.

Before he was taken to the cells, Wilver asked one more question.

'What's Sam going to do now?' he said. But he did not seem to expect an answer.

Eliot felt very tired. He was glad the case was over. Except for Amanda Grant, he had seen enough of Forley's friends. The interview had left a very unpleasant taste in his mouth. Men like Wilver believed they could control everything. How could he seriously believe that Forley's death would solve his son's problems? Especially as Sam had loved Forley so much. Eliot felt very sorry for the boy. He knew that Wilver had really been thinking of himself. Love can be so blind, he thought.

He looked across the room. Bowen's head was bent over his notes, his dark curly hair hiding the black circles under his eyes. He had spent all night finishing Forley's diary. Eliot smiled to himself. He wondered how long it would be before Bowen phoned Linda Scott. Would she be free, and would she be interested in him? This time maybe he would be lucky. Eliot hoped so. But in life you could never be sure of anything.